for Sister & George in friendship, appreciation
Mee Clemente

SWEETER THAN VIVALDI

LV

Along the long,
Cavatta pase:
Brown Cistercians
chanting matins.

("From A Bagman's Log,"
P. 64)

ALSO BY VINCE CLEMENTE

Poetry

Snow Owl Above Stony Brook Harbor (1977)
Songs from Puccini (1978)
Broadbill of Conscience Bay (1982)
Girl in the Yellow Caboose (1991)
This Shining Place (1992)
A Place for Lost Children (1997)
Watergaw (1998)
Tales from Concord:
Remembering Emerson, Thoreau, and Margaret Fuller
(forthcoming)
Starling in the Birdbath: The Sag Harbor Poems
(forthcoming)

Anthologies

From This Book of Praise (1978)
Paumanok Rising (1981)
John Ciardi: Measure of the Man (1987)
Remembering John Hall Wheelock (1991)

Autobiography

Under a Baleful Star: A Garland for Margaret Fuller
(forthcoming)

Vince Clemente

SWEETER THAN VIVALDI

Paintings by Ernesto F. Costa

Cross-Cultural Communications
New York / Kraków
2002

Paper Edition/ISBN 0-89304-673-6
Cloth Edition/ISBN 0-89304-672-8
Limited Edition/ISBN 0-89304-674-4

Editor-Publisher:
Stanley H. Barkan

Cross-Cultural Communications
239 Wynsum Avenue
Merrick, NY 11566-4725/USA
Tel: (001 516) 868-5635 / Fax: (001 516) 379-1901
E-mail: cccpoetry@aol.com

New York / Kraków 2002

First Edition

Produced in cooperation with:
Wydawnictwo Baran i Suszczyński
ul. Pijarska 5, 31-015 Kraków, Poland
Tel: (0048 12) 431 21 11 / Fax: (0048 12) 431 15 89
E-mail: wyd@wydbis.pl

Set by Wydawnictwo Baran i Suszczyński

Printed by Towarzystwo Słowaków w Polsce
Printed in Poland

For Peter Thabit Jones,
Welsh poet, friend, and man of Swansea

Americans acquire the habit of always considering
themselves as standing alone, and they are apt to
imagine that their whole destiny is in their hands....
[This] threatens in the end to confine him entirely
within the solitude of his own heart.
　　　　　—Alexis de Tocqueville
　　　　Democracy in America, 1835

It is, indeed, a complex fate being an American.
　　　　　—Henry James

It isn't that I am L'Italiano dirazzato, *though I*
guess I am. Though I also know I am not. I have
poured out endless poems about the Italian
"roots." Yet Jefferson, Tom Paine, and even—God
save the mark, Emerson—are as much at the roots
of my mind and feeling as the It. *of my* Am.
　　　　　—John Ciardi
　　　　Letter to Vince Clemente
　　　　November 10, 1978

CONTENTS

ART BY ERNESTO F. COSTA

Cover: *The Concert*

PREFACE:
SAFE IN THE CREEL OF THE EAR

I begin with the screech of the New Utrecht El, sparks dropping to the pavement below like moondust, and my diminutive mother, *Rosie*, calling me home through early *summer evenings* (a twelve year old, I would never violate my curfew), *Buddy, Buddy, Buddy.* I include my last *Hail Mary*, before falling off to sleep; the *sweetgum*, the lone tree in the tenement courtyard; my father *Louie* wedging *black eels* in a scale as the sun comes up above Fulton Market; the secret pleasure of the *I Love a Mystery* radio program, evenings, huddled in front of the old Emerson; the chestnut hair of *Marcy Monteverdi*, my first serious crush, the flickering shadow of curl along her *cheek*; my sixth-grade teacher, *Bridget Murphy*, who all but extinguished my wick of self-respect; my first encounter with death, the mangled corpse of my best friend, *Nelson Rossi*, the luckless boy having plummeted six stories to the street below, tracking his homing pigeons in their *rickety* coop, a perilous corner of tenement roof in Bensonhurst, Brooklyn. I begin with the long *E* sound, that primal *melody* as ubiquitous and *sweet* as birdsong, my unswerving companion, *steady* and always, through the Brooklyn *streets* of my boyhood, and now, all these years and lives later, undersong in my poems.

I believe Robert Frost says it best in his essay, "The Sound of Sense" (the piece grew out of letters home from England, 1912-1915, to friends like John Bartlett and Sidney Cox), when he concludes:

> *Just as many sounds belong to man as just so many vocal runs belong to one kind of bird. We come into the world with them and create none of them. What we feel as creation is only selection and grouping. We summon them from heaven knows where under excitement with the audial imagination.*

I'm convinced *I came into the world* with the baggage of the long *E* sound lodged in my racial ear, and that I've spent much of my life *grouping* it with other resonant, however minor, notes to make poems. A useless, self-absorbed way to live, most would say; and they may be right. However, something in me feels otherwise; and in this modest excursion, I would like to track this *audial* gift—*from Heaven knows where*—in a single poem in this volume, the last one I wrote in England in a village about 30 miles south of Beaconsfield, and the Frost family home, a modest cottage, end of Reynolds Road, just below an *eerie* pond.

I completed "At Night and in Trouble Sleep" just before leaving England in 1998, in that monk's cell of a study of mine, in our tilting cottage above the Thames. Reading it again, I can count at least 20 long *E* sounds; here's the full poem:

At night and in troubled *sleep*
I will ask my dead mother
to call *me* again through *the* lamp-lit *streets*
stand in the doorway, chaste and *lovely*
as if death had *merely* blanched her *cheek*
nudged her along the darkening hall
her tentative steps, *slipstream*
to the bracing caul of *mortality*
pleached around her.

Dark face of my darkest *dreams*
plover cawing along the *quay*,
the hundred other names I wake with
on my lips, febrile and stammering:
please, stand in the doorway chaste
and *lovely*, call *me* home, now *hurry*
back to the room, the *leaning* sill
the courtyard and a lone *tree*
sweetgum, if I remember, as I will

and then a room
within a room
where only longing is.

And why so many? I can't recall anything I've ever written with such a salient runnel of melody, indeed, a struck tuning fork, an unintentional *passacaglia*. And why not: a "dark" poem, the speaker indeed, in "trouble," at the end of his days—his "rope"—(the long *E* sound a "rope" through the labyrinth that was England)—and adrift, his very talk, "stammering." To be saved from this, the life of an "inner émigré," as Seamus Heaney called it, to be called "through the lamp-lit streets" and by his boy's name, *BuddEEEEEEE, BuddEEEEEEE*, and by a mother recently dead, her gait, the very "*slipstream*" of life, a counter-current she willed to the boy. Or simply this: the human cry from Adam down, the articulated *pain and joy of existence*, its very "longing" and *motions of grace*. I read the poem, recently, to an audience in Sag Harbor, my first public reading since our return from England, and found myself rocking as I said the thing, relinquishing as I did to its primal, gravitational tug.

I pray my reader find such song and solace in this volume, that comes to rest—and safe for now—in the very creel of the ear.

—Vince Clemente

May, 2001
Sag Harbor, New York

SNOW WALK, EARLY MORNING

You must try to understand
the deep wonder of it:
blue-cold of morning
a field stretching to the horizon

then to come upon
an owl's wingprint
in the snow, length
of a man's body.

The saints know:
traces and shadows of God,
even now
in such a time.

BLUE EYE TO GREEN EYE

Would you believe!
Picking strawberries at Lewin Farm
just west of Wading River,
there under blossom and leaf
I grabbed for one—size of my fist,
and ... would you believe
it flew away but so close
it brushed my cheek to flame
eye to eye: blue eye
to my green.

A redwing!
And ... would you believe
it found the meadowfence
that said the farm's end
and lingered
then cawed at me
as if it knew my name:
Vincent   Vincent
Vincent—
would you believe?

THE MARTYRDOM OF SAVONAROLA: 1498

While Lorenzo lay dying in his villa at Careggi
dreaming of Michelangelo's *Faun*,
you from your pulpit in the Duomo
decreed, *Viva Cristo!*

Christ, King of Florence,
and warned Lorenzo's city
to wash its whored flesh in the Arno,
to wait the judgment of an angry God.

You, the green-man
in Bartolomeo's *Portrait*,
a stranger from the north,
uneasy among these Florentines.

In the end you proved too much for them.
The flames from your toad-gray vestments
lit up the Piazza Vecchio
as your maimed body

crunched to ash: splintered bones
of a fickle sparrow driven to earth
by an impatient boy from the hillside country,
with his crudely made slingshot.

PUCCINI AT TORRE DEL LAGO

Your arm rudders
the cold lake water,
as your rifle lolls,
propped among the decoys.
You spy a lone widgeon bank,
flirt with the tideline.

In the morning's fawnlight
you remember the dead child,
her breast heaving,
poison racing to the brain:
one last star of light
behind her eyelid.

> *Never go to the fen, my child,*
> *never to the fen*
> *a bird flew there*
> *and lost its wings,*
> *your dreamer-father has not been seen,*
> *your mother, taken by the gypsies.*

In the bait-shack
lost in the swamp alder,
a woman bends over a grate
turns a lake bass over
stirs polenta in a copper bucket,
then stops to blow a kiss.

You swear you smell
the fragrance
of her hair,
feel her hand,
tremble
along your ribcage.

An old man
you understand
the rail's hoarse cry,
the slant of last light
along your back,
hear the child's song again:

>*Never go to the fen, my child,*
>*never to the fen*
>*a bird flew there*
>*and lost its wings,*
>*your dreamer-father has not been seen,*
>*your mother, taken by the gypsies.*

NONNA TAKING LEAVE

I imagine her last walk through the hibiscus
    grove
from the veranda of the stone house her father
    built
and knowing her, as I think I do,
fingering her beads, the *Sorrowful Mysteries*,
    all the while
praying to the god along her shoulder, wandering
in the theater leaning perilously on a cliff.

The time now, a century and a half later, closing
down on my own days, a story
wedged in the *Part Called Age*, I find myself
where Etna runnels to sea, landsend,
my own mad blood stirred to bless or curse
a Sicilian light Nonna never relinquished.

Bruno, local ghost and friendly ruin,
be with me, lattice my song
with the shepherd pipe's heartbreak
Nonna sang to my mother,
and goat milk, the udder full enough
to appease forever the thirst for things I carry

in the grotto of the heart, rest
now in my sixth decade, trust
whatever the heart's yearning brings: life's skein

is here, its disparate watermark in place,
   the diurnal turning
our story, Nonna, like Bruno before her, the one
with deft hands, nimble fingers,

like the dawning: chaste, true, and full of grace.

AN ITALIAN ODYSSEY: 1892

You swear you're back in Rositana
feel the late-day sun along your neck
as you trace a skein of railroad track
stretching east to Mississippi
that seems to undulate in afternoon haze,
too hot, even in shade of the boss's shack.

You are 15, Uncle Joseph, stand
hands in pockets, numb.
Your father's arm around you
is little comfort.
You've never seen him cry before, at 15,
you're too old to cry, too old.

The word *Wop* didn't rile you,
you heard that before,
nor the way the drunken foreman
looked at you
through broken teeth.
But this is something else:

Six months laying track
from Shreveport to the Mississippi line
across half of Louisiana,
on payday, the shack boarded,
they leave a sign reading,
Out To Lunch!

How you got back to New York City,
the tiny walk-up,
white-washed flat,
without a dime in your pocket
with red-dust in your hair,
that part my mother forgets.

All your life, though,
you remember your father sobbing,
on his knees, sobbing,
Sweet Christ!
How will we tell Mama,
tell Mama?

MONROE STREET, NEW YORK CITY: 1900

"Crazy!" is all he can say.
"The flat's not small enough,
you must partition off
half the kitchen!"

Behind the makeshift wall
a spread bleached
the color of bone, whatever
you were able to carry from Rositana:

Your father's mandolin
and earthen pots hang
from gray walls, chaste,
untouched.

Each night you scrub them,
Grandma Antonina.
You never wanted to come
to America.

Why should a woman
leave her home, a veranda
that runneled to the sea.
Yet always, Calogero inisted.

"Restless," your mother called him.
"Too curious about

what was beyond mountains,"
she warned.

At night, you huddle
near the kerosene burner,
sip chamomile tea
and scrub the earthen pots.

You swear you hear
the mandolin's sweet strain, smell
fig blossoms, see the almond
bloom early this spring.

FROM THE ARDEATINE CAVES

Nazi war criminal Herbert Kappler, 71, former police chief of Rome, died yesterday of stomach cancer. He had been serving a life term for the execution of 335 Italians, mostly Jews, in reprisal for the ambush killing of 32 German soldiers by Italian partisans in Rome. The execution was staged in the Ardeatine Caves, just outside of Rome. German engineers assisted in sealing the caves that entombed the victims. The execution was carried out on 24 March 1944, now observed as a national day of mourning.
—*The New York Times*, February 1978

I. Above the Giardino alla Francese

From your window above the Giardino alla
    Francese
you muse through cypress groves
to the pond, the footbridge
and think of Monet at Giverny—
the water lilies like floating candles.

From your window above the Giardino alla
    Francese
you record in meticulous columns
your *Todeskandidaten*,
these "candidates for death"
for the order that read:

"Ten Italians for every German dead
in today's ambush."

You've been up all night
listening to Wagner
remembering your boyhood in Stuttgart,
at 6 AM a vireo's song woke you
to the list incomplete—
and you had run out of Jews.

True, you have no stomach for this, Herr Kappler,
but a soldier like a monk
takes his solemn vows,
and out of some misty logic
you tell yourself
that what you are doing
is God's work—
a god, red-eyed
all in pieces,
feeding the fall harvest.

II. Inside the Ardeatine Caves

You learn, Herr Kappler,
how one of your young officers
refused to shoot:
he looked too deeply
into the eyes of a boy,
the baker's helper from Rimini,
and saw for a second
his own brother
home from Dresden.
He could not fire;
the pistol froze
at the boy's temple.

At the bottom of the hill
you think you smell death,
only mountain ash:
berries hemorrhaging in the heat.
The young officer is there,
tentative at the cave's mouth,
double-lightning bolt
on his helmet, gleams.

"Better I at your side
when you fire," you say,
then walk him
arm about waist
into the chamber.

Once inside, it is easy,
the cognac helps—
even the baker's helper falls.

The bodies are piled in rows
stacked like bread
and the caves are sealed tight.

"No resurrection here,"
you tell yourself,
as you light a cigarette,
"no, none tonight."

TERESA GULLACE, IN MEMORIAM: MARCH 2, 1944

Teresa Gullace, pregnant, thirty-seven-year-old mother of five children, was killed by a German soldier, shot in the head, as she tried to throw a piece of bread to her imprisoned husband.
—Robert Katz, *Death in Rome*

No one heard the gunshot.
It could have been the Fiat
parked near the barracks
backfiring,
it could have been.

They found you
pinned to the fence
sobbing,
the sixth child stunned
in your womb
praying for light.
You clutched the piece of bread
still warm,
wrapped in your kerchief.

All you saw in the Roman night
was the double-lightning bolt
on his helmet,
the face of a boy
no older than your eldest son.

All you wanted
was that your husband
have a piece of bread
with his evening pasta.
That's all you wanted,
bread for his pasta.

FATHER OF THE DAUGHTERS, ASSASSINATED

You refuse their blindfold
take one final look
at the Dolomites
only peaks are seen
through morning haze.

What you think these final moments
we'll never know:
maybe your young wife
buried in the churchyard
near the belltower, maybe
the child left behind in America,
the child I married, or the one
quiet in the nursery.

But I'm sure you heard a wood thrush,
the bell waking the monks
in the monastery at Gemona.
I'm sure you crossed yourself
as they gave signal
to raise weapons and take aim.

Not twenty feet away
you saw one as the boy
who poured your coffee
in the Rimini Caffé,

the one who talked about football,
looked like the son
you never had.

Now you are a skull in his gunsight,
as he jerks the trigger and fires,
as the bullet enters.
Your crown rends:
breastbone of a singing bird
hums in the windfall,
the bullet comes to rest
in the spine of a poplar.

You were named Umberto
after the Crown Prince.
All your life
you followed such a one:
your devotion to *Il Duce*,
the photo of the two of you
swimming in the Adriatic,
your staying
after all had fled
to Switzerland.

The door ajar,
you sit in the wicker chair
and read Malaparte.
As they enter you say,

"Don't wake the child
sleeping in the nursery."

The war is long over,
Italy survives without a king.
The boy in the Rimini Caffé
is an old man, many times
blessed, and prospers:

He never talks about such things.

STORY OF THE ORPHANS

The Roman day about to break
above the hills, the quiet time,
yet bosoms heave sighs along the kitchen
table ricochet, *le sorelle*
enact the ancient ritual of loss,

the old War suddenly
a skirmish in the back yard. Listen
as the hill people plunder the farmhouse,
now the marriage bed, and underfoot
a fading wedding dress.

Only the child, the crib freshly scrubbed,
is left and a fascist father
stammering to prayer, so the story goes,
as Christina, the child and sole survivor
sobbing, recalls with the heart's

scar-tissue of memory
almost too sad to call back
from those dark hills
that dark night: first
the pounding on the door

and the father too proud
to cower, "Don't wake the child,
Don't wake her! No! not at this hour!"
And then the procession
like mendicant friars to the leaning

copper beech, the bark piercing
his thigh until it is salmon-glazed.
Christina shakes; Nina can't stop her sobbing,
the volley of shots, an upgust:
how like thunder through the mountains.

And then, and then ... the corpse is left to rot;
no one dare resist the *partigiani*
until the young priest, alone, drags the father
to the churchyard, a sack of meal
propped between his young bride,

dead at 24, and the stunted rowan bush.
Like those who linger, hang-on
after a friendly wake, we will stop to pause,
bless the dead, comfort the dying in us.
The sisters will part, the one

left here in Rome, where it is always sunny,
and the convallaria bloom, the other
to a tilting house above the Thames,
mornings, she'll find the dove's-neck lustre
dancing in the bunt of her skirt.

And the mad father, who refused to run,
left a bundle of soiled shirts,
will rest for now, here
under their blanched eyelids
where it is always dark.

MOTHER SONG

From the lone sweetgum
arched in the tenement courtyard
I am a camera eye
in a yellow blossom, hanging
from star-veined leaves,
following a young girl,
my mother at 20
the age of my daughters,
ironing worker's shirts
in soft morning light
that folds a ghostly shawl
around her
as she sings to me
rocking in her small womb.

She is lithe and dark
like a farmgirl
up from the fields
carrying hayricks
into the barn
before a late-day storm,
her girl's body rent
by the first wingbar of dusk
above the lavender mountains,
as under her
heaving,
the earth's dark heart.

AT NIGHT AND IN TROUBLED SLEEP

At night and in troubled sleep
I will ask my dead mother
to call me again, through the lamp-lit streets,
stand in the doorway, chaste and lovely
as if death had merely blanched her cheek
nudged her along the darkened hall
her tentative steps, slipstream
to the bracing caul of mortality
pleached around her.

Dark face of my darkest dreams
plover cawing along the quay,
the hundred other names I wake with
on my lips, febrile and stammering:
please, stand in the doorway chaste
and lovely, call me home, now hurry
back to the room, the leaning sill,
the courtyard and a lone tree
sweetgum, if I remember, as I will

and then a room
within a room
where only longing is.

REMEMBERING MA ON A COLD MORNING

for William Stafford

Morning thaw: first the old Chevy, then the Cove
the lone merganser, scudding an icefloe.
My heart breaks, evanescent as wind,
the soft caul of morning rends, *not your last*,
    I'm sure.

There was a time (memory, hold, please hold)
when Ma steered the clothesline
to a tree, shadows—back in the courtyard,
a child, I'd ask, *But, Ma, where does it end?*

Why, in heaven, she'd say, certain
as grace was certain, then;
her face, a saint's sweetness,
and wiser than God's.

That world, my mother's,
is all but gone:
a mote, adrift somewhere,
a sunspot in a dark well.

In the morning thaw
the clothesline snaps,
how to get
to heaven?

FOUR VIEWS OF A FATHER

I. Newark Airport, July 1973

A son & his father
two men pissing;
the older man shy,
his back in shadows,
hides his manhood.

The younger one
wanting to say, *Come, Pop,
here at my side,
let's piss at the stars,
put out the heavens' fires.*

God! How slow love moves.

II. Father Dream

The packer's hook floats above the scale
in the briny dream of Fulton Market
I drift with to find my father

who is the figure in an old photo,
a boy really,
the age of my daughters.

He raises the hook
that has become his right hand
and drowns it in a salmon barrel,

then raises it again: prongs squint
in the fish's eye
through its pink heart.

His arm arched skyward,
so high
it is starbruised.

The fish rocks in the scale's belly
as if alive, as if the hook's blow
woke it from sleep.

He smiles in green coveralls
tied with monkshemp at the waist
and looks to me, his son

to kiss his eyes open,
to take his hand,
that is the hand of a worker.

The one nail blue from a hammer-blow
like an indigo bunting
throbs under my thumb

as we walk the cobblestones of South Street
and see the market's scales tilt to the moon,
silver, then blue again.

III. My Father's Seine

In the corner
by the shipwright's chest,
and rising like a hayrick,
my father's seine is sleeping,

dreams the shadrun
down from Maine
the alewives
gliding in the headwaters,

feels the river's chill
along the old man's wrists
a caress so soft
it trembles, so soft ...

Yet, I have only dreamed this
and should know better.
The rick is a headstone
leaning, a cemetery in Queens,

the shadrun, salmon
squirming in a scale
as dawn comes above
Fulton Market.

Christ! How that man
held that scale!
Galileo in all his wisdom
could not have done it better:

With a fulcrum
he balanced the world.
Papa, I give it back to you:
shafts of opal-light

along the market,
the startled quay
now salmon-glazed,
shimmering.

IV. Father to Son: Last Words

I've been told
  my father's last words
    coughing blood, syllables

adrift in his throat:
  The cold, oh, the cold,
    please, some hot water

a comforter,
  the oil heating
    on the kerosene stove,

my dead mother's shroud,
  sweet Christ—
    anything.

Papa, I'm late again,
  but here, lean on me,
    slide along my hip,

place your hand
  under my shirt
    where it's warm,

the other one
  round the nape of my neck,
    now hold on.

I'm strong, Papa,
 toss away your stave,
   look: we're almost home.

STARLING IN THE BIRDBATH

The light along its neckplate
just where the sun
broke through cedar-lace
lit the kitchen
like the mornings of childhood
those tinctured with grace,
the lilac-light of elevated train
that chugged above the bedroom window
and the boy who called, *Lord, you here—
in this place?*

I'm certain it was that light
that glaze along creation's face
ambling along the kitchen wall
as the starling preened, then bowed
the way a mendicant lowers his eyes
just before prayer time
and decade after decade
until the beads worn to dust
crumble in his hands, the words
an alphabet of ash, bittersweet taste.

I tell this at this century's end
and at troubled peace,
certain that the starling
unaware of his role in this story
is already off somewhere
in the legend of his own life

and has found his way without me
in a world far better than mine.

I pray he forgives this incursion
this human-tinkering and butting-in,
so like my kind:
always this thumb-print we leave behind
that shouts, *I'm here,*
I'm here! yet rarely asks,
But where are you?
May I touch your face?

THE BOY, THE DROPPED CALF

The pitchfork
at rest in hay
dreams in afternoon graindust.

I am 15
a Fresh-Air kid
on loan from the city,
and see for the first time
a barn owl in the hickory beams,
the loft a cathedral
I will never leave.

In the stall below,
the placenta broken,
birth-vapors rise
from the mother's teats.

I hear the calf drop
see its vein's blue-light
fill the barn's darkest corners,
feel an angel kiss my lips:

Her breath
smells
of jasmine.

LEAFLIGHT

It has followed me
all the way to *here*:
found me in the first
lengthening evening of spring,
the sweetgum's leaflight,
chrysoprase along the courtyard
and the shadow of cloud-cover
skittering across the quay.

It says: place your ear
above the harp in the ribcage
and listen to its runnel of inexorable song,
it never lies.

What is it, but the lazy ooze
and fording silence
that certain passacaglia
of time.

HOPKINS FISHES THE ELWY

for Peter Thabit Jones

The creel leaned in the thicket,
rickety, too modest for sound;
the line cloud-drifted its way to the outbank
and sank, neither ripple nor root
pockmarked the surface,
the cast was that perfect, only
a long *wisp* and *slip*: the sound of some daft
    insect.

The morning too early for matins, dawn's
flickering wingbar along his shoulder,
and with the heart's ivy-patience
he waited, certain a trout would take the fly,
already feeling the tug of the line, the ever-so-
slight winch in the wrist, so much like that time
between the raising of the Host

and the breathless taking in.

THOREAU PACKS HIS JOURNALS

Like a child carrying
the first spring flowers
from a dark wood
into the sudden light
of a New England morning,
you pile the slim volumes,
already tottering, a mason
building a wall
that will last forever.

You mortise the four dozen or so
snugly in the white-spruce box,
catch your breath
and pause to hear
in a gust through spruce-bough
a loon's call
across the mizzling lake,
the sudden lurch of the early train
in from Boston.

You wedge spaces with alpine moss
until the box, like a coffin
is airtight, then drag it
screeching to the wall
alongside the cane daybed
down from your attic room
to the family parlor
where you'll take
your final look at things.

A surveyor to the end
you want to sound, to measure
the depths of all you love in Concord:
a family already rent by death,
only mother Cynthia
and sister Sophia are left,
and, of course, all the maiden aunts.
Your life to the very end
is women-centered.

And all that's left now
is to wait for Death.
You'll know this for sure:
He'll come out of the woods
hiking boots flecked with hematite
a trillium dangling from his earlobe.
He'll sit by the fire
sip birch tea, and won't leave,
until you give in to sleep,

until your eyes are closed
and waters glide
under your eyelids,
porting you downstream
to a cove
where spartina hassocks
hold the sun,
solemn
like wheat fields.

CLAMMING AT DUSK
for William Heyen

I

At low tide, prongs of my clamrake
sing under burning stars.

I disturb a world underfoot
probing for chowders.

Musselpools like obsidian
blink through sawgrass,

as I probe, prongs of the clamrake
make old stone music

under watching stars.
In the distance, a willet

its wings strung across
the bluff, on fire.

At dusk, the Sound settles
into dumb silence, no sound

save the whisper of my clamrake:
prongs now my own fingers

enter the belly of mudflat,
darkness pulls me in

fingers scale the surface
of seacaves, over the face

of eternal places, ageless
like the silence of the ocean's floor.

II

The flatboat at anchor rocks,
I wake it from sleep

nudge it into darkness, head back
to Stony Brook Harbor.

With only stars for eyes we glide,
oarlocks crack in evening stillness

downshaft of oar, my hand:
the black Sound stings, cupped fingers

gather kelp and seamoss, grow numb
and clutch the bushel of chowders.

Oars at rest, I ride current
burrow through cattails:

They brush against the boat, whisper
not yet, not yet, not yet.

We rise, as if out of dreams
out of bur reeds, stalks along

the dark channel like girls swaying
fingers pressed to lips.

Sighting shore, the grist mill
its stone wheel dumb:

Blue mussels hang like autumn grapes
about to burst.

III

Flatboat beached
I lug the evening's harvest to shore,

chowders fall like moondust
lie nacreous in black sand.

Press one to my lips:
brim of the clam stings

briny sweetness in my mouth.
Pull from my pocket a knife

and shuck the chowder, run my
fingers over its scalloped cheek:

ageless, silent like the walls
of seacaves: old as stone.

FLYFISHING

He casts his taut line
through a flock of Canada geese
the way a woodcutter
splits a hickory log
with a single blow,
the line as straight as truth,
the snap a broadbill's purr
across the thawing April snow.

I hold my breath,
pray the bite never comes,
the trout stay close
to the pond's floor,
hear this island's ancient song:
the billion-year-old melody
along the glacial moraine.

FROM A BAYMAN'S LOG

I

Such a morning!
Even the sandcrab sleeps.
From my garvey, a line:
It falls
ten thousand years.

II

Twenty below:
blackice
dark as obsidian.

Little Africa
a lilac bird
dreams a warm current
the Gulf of Mexico.

III

Night will not let go!
I move through the dark this morning:
an eel's blue eye
my jacklight.

IV

Along the Bay
Canada geese:
Brown Cistercians
chanting matins.

V

Such tenderness!
Sea and sky copulate
wild lavender sigh.

VI

After a night's rain
the Bay, a pregnant dolphin
preens in morning haze.

VII

I like the way the sun rises
above the post office:
first, endtips of a blue tamarack,
then the weathervane man-of-war,
bronze as November blood
straining at its moorings.

I hear the crew, their heartbreak:
such a morning, such a morning,
they say.

VIII

Mid-day, my clamrake
sings along Little Africa

wakes the canvasback
sleeping in the mudflats.

IX

A gust across the Sound!
I hear the woodcutter in Maine
bless his axe-handle,

the tamarack fall,
the oven bird
shake in its nest.

X

The bell from Grace Church
swings in my heart tower:
I drop my net
seine for the dead
asleep in seacaves.

DEER IN THE ORCHARD

Like me
  they cannot sleep
    rise out of the woods

light as mist
  along vein-leaf,
    waking to morning.

See
  how they bend:
    on their spotted backs

matted glacial-fern,
  hepatica-
    leaf

as they poke
  through the undergrowth
    and glean.

Lord,
  not a single
    winesap is safe.

SEASON OF MARRIAGE
for John Ciardi

I

At the mountain pass
we turned to pick up the lives
we left below in the valley,
but you gathered at random,
so I thought, wildflowers
wrapped in ferncloth
snug in your hand
shaped by the love you have for small things,
bigger things, too.

There! you said,
as you placed the last blue sailor
alongside the mountain pink
then raised the bunch
above your head, far above
the mountain's crest,
the way a priest
raises the Host
intones the word
Miracle.

For a moment it looked as though
some mountain god
daft on morning air
had placed in the mountain's hair

a bouquet of flowers
and ran off, afraid to look,
too shy: as shy as a girl
bathing in a mountain brook,
clothes hang from boughs
of trembling hawthorn.

II

We wake to find the March snow-melt
   so high, the old house founders
      a gray ship, bottom of the Sound.

But, Annie, as we slept
   a new star was born: see
      the star-bruise above your breast.

III

I light the lamp now
find you undressing,
the flame splays your breasts
yor midriff, the inside
of a shimmering conch.
Sweet thing, I will hold you against me
as your thighs, tapers,
candle my groin.

These are the thoughts of a man
in the husbandry of his days.
The woman undressing is his wife,
the light her heart-candle,
the room above an inland dune
end of Orient Point:
The light so pure
it is seen in Portugal.

IV

Annie, the redpoll's back,
hear its raspy song.
It found the downy spot
under the hip
of the English holly.

Look: in its eyes
the blue arctic,
spiraling wastes that spread
beyond the earth's shell, empty
into Vega's breastplate.

But imagine
the swell,
the swarm
and throng
of dripping
stars.

V

On the windowsill
the saucepan you left to cool
leans in starlight.

But look:
In the frothing kettle soup
a nova tears itself away,
a galaxy is born.
Christ! I'm just a castaway,
but in your eyes,
so help me,
all of time's geologic story.

VI

In your arms you clutch
the zinnia harvest
the farmchild cut
in a field
high above the Sound,
petal-tips already seared
with autumn: mauve,
night-blue, russet-brown.

The night upon us, Annie,
we'd better go.
It comes a black-faced lamb
that finds us in shadows

just below the timberline,
then runs its mouth along our thighs—
but look: the longing,
oh, such longing, there
in its eyes.

VII

We could not see
the mountains through the snow,
even the soft yellow glow,
the kitchen in the gray house
we love so
is lost in snow-mist.

Was it carried off
in the arms of a snowstar
to the river of dark-shoaled light?
Does it ride a current, bob
this way or that?

Is that you, Annie,
with me, two old people
holding hands, lost
in whorls of pinedust
across the kitchen table,

knees braced
for one last journey:
travelers
our name.

MATTITUCK

"Beyond the far field
the picking's best,"
the farmchild said
half to herself
half to Annie and me.

We followed her eye's line
to a meadow of aster
and columbine
and found the field
by its strawberry scent—
but didn't stop there.

Snared in the tidepull
we walked another quarter
mile or so to a dunepath
yellow in afternoon haze,
pausing to rest
in the shade
of a cypress bough.

While below
in the Sound's
still waters,
a family of dolphin
preening: blue
then green again.

God! How they loved
one another.

SOGNO D'ORO

At the mountain pass at dusk, breathless
you take my hand and tell me
how a child, she'd sit all day
and listen to that melody on a roller-piano,
hair tied under a gold-straw hat,
feet beating wildly on the pedals, her eyes
starlings, dart to places beyond the hills,
she never heard her mother call.

Why have you waited until now
to tell me this, about the mother
you never knew, herself a child and far away,
long asleep in a Tuscan churchyard?
Now I see how she passed on to you
and our daughters, this darkness,
so dark, the stars' luminous
pauses, cannot lighten.

Was it the song I hummed
driving through the mountains?
It was her song, you said, the one
that followed her to evening-prayer, footfalls
along the burnished tiles.
Please, dearheart, say it—this once more
before I break in two: *Sogno D'oro* ...
Golden Dream.

(Marzo   primavera
sgelo di neve,
tempo per ricordare.)

March   spring
snow thawing,
time for remembering.

DAUGHTER AT THE SEVEN SISTERS SCHOOL

Women shuttle by in cowls
like dour monks,
in battle fatigues
their gray skin keeps
a sleepy Pennsylvania morning
at bay.

I pray for color:
the child's blue translucent
veinswell as it drops
from its mother's womb,
cinnamon eggs rocking
on the pinegrove floor,
fresh-pink impatiens
forsaking their windowbox lives
for heaven, gold flecks
on the perch's back,
the sun easing into the pond.

And you, my daughter,
rise from a clump of birch
in terracotta shoes, in a dress
of orange and red nasturtium:
You are a flowerbed!

The rose-tint of dawn returned,
the bloodflow, the blush

in the young girl's face.
My fatherhood presses on me
rises, lives in this

in this place.

FOR A DAUGHTER FAR FROM HOME

I imagine how, from your bedroom window,
You see Tsukuba through mist
rising from rice fields,
wake to a farmer's call
pitched high above birdsong,
strain for the Japanese word
for the bird whose wingbar
is color of the spartina meadow
along our harbor: a place
we know as home.

I remember how you ran through leaves
high as hayricks:
You liked the crimson dogwood best,
(always the first to go), then
the yellow sassafras,
pausing to speak to something:
Our little mystic, we said.
Now I know: Why is it then
I never told you, my daughter?

Gina, I've been up all night
reading Stryk's translations from the Zen,
and there's one poem I come back to
again and again,
one I know you'd like,
about an old monk
lost in sudden rain

and at day's end,
with tree colors darkening,
then weeps, not knowing where the monastery is.

And then he hears
the bonging of bells
feels in his wispy bones
the clay fire rising in his cell,
the path under him
a way home:
all steady and now.

Gina, think of us when mist wreathes Tsukuba,
and if you find an old monk
in an orange robe,
one who has strayed too far
in the rain from his cell,
take his hand and call him, *Father.*
In his eyes you'll find
the child braiding leaves in her hair,
who understood the diurnal turning,
the soft omphalos we walk upon.

SEGOVIA PLAYING VILLA LOBOS

From the screened-in porch
laughter of my wife and daughters
and Segovia playing Villa Lobos.

I move through shadows
quilting the yard,
float along the glacial moraine,

remember the haul seiners
of the Great South Bay:
how stars fell into their silver nets

their skiffs
dreamed in the tideswell,
how their sighs

broke the heart
of a plover
nesting in the sand strawberry.

Lord, my Lord, I'd Like
to hold this moment forever, quiet,
in the bunt of the heart.

BELLAGIO

The bells of the hilltop church
seine the tideline
as a monk jerks the bellcord
shivers under his tunic
that is green like the mountain.

He does not know where the bellnotes settle
or who wakes to smile
or frown at the delicate sound,
he does not see the lovers turn in their sleep
nor the mother light a candle for her dead child.

He knows the goshawk riding a furrow of cloud
leaves a long, deep shadow
that covers the mountain, so deep
even winter will not erase,
and that the earth's mensural heart

drones a steady passacaglia
as it will tomorrow
as it did yesterday
and even later,
after hushed evensong.

The bell pitted by time
the mensural clock flickering,
what do they mean to the lizard
drinking deftly from the convallaria
outside the Church of the Martyred Saints?

HAYING

Laved in heat and chaff-dust
I raise the forked bundle
high above my head, find
the beckoning corner
where first light finds me
wakeful as grace.

Total attention is prayer, I would learn
years and years later;
but that time, haying,
I worked alone, the barn
a cathedral I would never leave,
nor ever find again.

Now I know, I've done nothing as right
as the boy's haying in a loft
above a stall, chewing on timothy, tracking
cowbells in the drizzly morning
waiting for his mother's call.
Oh, that never came.

Days rushing to compline,
a wintry thing, I'll enter the loft again
that stall of night
where it is never dark,
where the boy still kneels
hushed, in suppliant devotion.

He'll teach me the arc of flight
of the hurtling bale, the comet's curve
and certainty of destination,
the steady omphalos we walk upon.

He'll steady me
and point to our new home:
Old chums, we'll jostle, banter,
track cowbells along the way.

ACKNOWLEDGMENTS

Some of these poems first appeared in *American Literary Review*, *Berkeley Poetry Review*, *Bluefish*, *Blue Unicorn*, *Convergence*, *Images*, *Italian Americana* (University of Rhode Island), *Live Poets Society Anthology*, *The Ledge*, *Long Island Quarterly*, *Long Pond Review*, *New Virginia Quarterly*, *Street Magazine*, *VIA* (Purdue University), and *Wetlands*. "Flyfishing" was first published in the broadside series, *Portfolio One/ 1983* (The Stone House Press); "Clamming at Dusk" first appeared in the anthology, *On Good Ground* (Street Press, 1980); "The Boy, the Dropped Calf," "Daughter at the Seven Sisters School," "Teresa Gullace: In Memoriam," and "Story of the Orphans" were first published in *A Place for Lost Children* (Karma Dog Editions, 1998); "The Martyrdom of Savonarola: 1498," "Monroe Street, New York City: 1900," and "Father of the Daughters, Assassinated" were first published in *Songs from Puccini* (Four Rivers Press, 1978); "Bellagio" and "At Night and in Troubled Sleep" first appeared in *Watergaw Along the Thames* (Birnham Wood Graphics, 1998); "From the Ardeantine Caves" was first published in the anthology, *Blood to Remember: American Poets on the Holocaust*, edited by Charles Fishman (Texas Tech University Press, 1991).

ABOUT THE ARTIST

Ernesto F. Costa was born in Brooklyn, New York, in 1926 to immigrant parents from Northern Italy. He showed an early aptitude and love for art, winning prizes in school and throughout his professional life. At Lincoln High School, he came under the influence of the brilliant teacher, Leon Friend, who saw in his student, along with a rare talent, one "destined to go places." Costa continued his education at Black Mountain College in Ashville, North Carolina, and Pratt Institute in New York. His early career was dedicated to the commercial arts as art director in advertising agencies (including Grey Advertising) and as art editor of *House & Garden* and *Interior* magazines. Costa's work is a blend of both the intellectual and passionate view of the world. His most recent paintings present a mystical world where wit and celebration of the life-force transcend human suffering and triumph over darkness. Costa has exhibited at the Lincoln Gallery, the Philadelphia Academy of Fine Arts, the Brooklyn Museum, the National Art League, the Grace Gallery, the Hutchins Gallery, the New York Catholic Center, the Parrish Art Museum, the Nassau County Museum of Art, and the Galerie Mistinguette. He is the recipient of awards from the American Institute of Graphic Arts and the International Film & TV Festival. He is represented in permanent collections in the Museum of Modern Art and the Library of Congress.

ART BY ERNESTO F. COSTA
IN THIS VOLUME

Cover: *The Concert*, 1992, oil on canvas, 16 x 20"

14 *Landscape*, 1988, oil on cnvas, 16 x 20"

21 *Sicilian Marionettes*, 1993, oil on canvas,
    18 x 24"

24 *The Arrangement*, 1991, oil on canvas,
    20 x 24"

50 *Taking Aim*, 1990, oil on canvas, 16 x 20"

61 *The Catch*, 1992, oil on canvas, 16 x 20"

66 *Geese Alarm*, 1978, oil on canvas, 20 x 24"

73 *Black Face*, 1933, watercolor on paper,
    18 x 19"

ABOUT THE AUTHOR

Vince Clemente, a SUNY English Professor Emeritus, is a poet-biographer, whose books include *John Ciardi: Measure of the Man* (University of Arkansas Press, 1987), *Paumanok Rising* (1981), and seven volumes of verse, one of which, *A Place for Lost Children* (1997), is a text used at the University of Wales at Swansea. His work has also appeared in *The New York Times*, *Newsday*, *The Boston Book Review*, *The South Carolina Review*, newspapers and other publications in the United Kingdom, as well as in anthologies like *Blood to Remember: American Poets on the Holocaust* (Texas Tech University Press) and *Darwin: A Norton Critical Third Edition*. As a visiting lecturer, he has spoken at Hofstra, CW Post, Southampton College, SUNY Albany, Oswego, as well as at museums like the Heckscher and Parrish. For many years a trustee of the Walt Whitman Birthplace and founding editor of *West Hills Review: a Walt Whitman Journal*, he has recently returned from two years in England, where he lectured and wrote. He now lives in Sag Harbor with his wife, Ann, and serves as a columnist for *The Sag Harbor Express*. *The Vince Clemente Papers* are now part of the Rush Rhees Library, Department of Rare Books & Collections of Rochester University.

SOME WORDS FOR VINCE CLEMENTE

"The poems speak so, heart to heart, pulse to pulse, ache to joyful ache of life, its beauty, its grief, its shimmer."
—*Karl Shapiro*

"And this is why you are one of our important writers: because your speaking voice, natural voice, is your writing voice, too. And this means you have earned, by a long life of integrity, such honesty that makes the rest of us listen hard."
—*William Heyen*

"In *This Shining Place*, like Hardy, Clemente brings off what are ostensibly clumsy coinages which shouldn't work—such as 'heart sextant'—and they become quite perfect in context, enriching a delicately graven and poignant achievement."
—*Paul Newman* (Cornwall, England)

"The values that the style and spirit of these poems imply and create are ones that I feel are especially needed, civilizing, and life-enhancing."
—*John Tagliabue*

"Vince Clemente is a rare spirit and a fine poet whose work is filled with tenderness and compassion. His work should be known to many, who will find that the poems are both moving and graceful, and fully expressive of the man."
—*Lucien Stryk*